LOVHERS

Picas Series 1

NICOLE BROSSARD

LOVHERS

Translated by Barbara Godard

GUERNICA

Copyright © 1980 by Nicole Brossard and Editions Quinze.
Translation © 1986 by Barbara Godard and Guernica Editions.
First published in this format in 1987.
All rights reserved.
Printed in Canada.
Guernica Editions and the Translator
gratefully acknowledge financial support
from the Canada Council and le Ministère
des Affaires culturelles du Québec.

Guernica Editions, P.O. Box 633, Station N.D.G.,
Montréal (Québec), Canada H4A 3R1

Legal Deposit — Third Quarter
Bibliothèque nationale du Québec & National Library of Canada.

Canadian Cataloguing in Publication Data

Brossard, Nicole, 1943-
(Amantes. English)
Lovhers

(Picas series; 1)
Translation of: Amantes.
ISBN 0-919349-93-5

I. Godard, Barbara.   II. Title.   III. Title: Amantes.   English.
IV. Series.

PS8503.R7A7213 1987   C84'.54   C87-090185-0
PQ3919.2.B76A7213 1987

Earlier versions of some of these poems were published in
Prism International, *Fireweed* and *Exile*. The translator grate-
fully acknowledges the work of Ray Ellenwood in editing the
translation.

Table of Contents

Preface

One could write a history of theories of translation, a history of the relationships between author and translator, indeed between author and reader, by writing a history of the preface as genre. Immediately, one would find oneself plunged in controversy, for the preface is commonly thought of as the translator's cardinal sin. It violates the current rule that a translation must not give the impression that it is a translation: it should present itself as a text native to the target language and conceal all signs of its transformation, even the translator's signature. An alternate theory of translation would attack this illusion of transparency by underlining the differences between two cultures and their linguistic systems and viewing the translated text as a conglomerate, not a unitary, structure. It would insist on translation as an act of reading, as an interpretation, one among many possible. Translation here is a practice of reading/writing and, as such, the historical adventure of a subject. The modest, self-effacing translator, corollary to the notion of tranparency, is replaced by a translator who is an active participant in the creation of meaning, and may even immodestly flaunt her signature — in a preface.

My intent is not to write that history, pertinent though it may be. I propose instead to share the trajectory of my particular reading of Nicole Brossard's *Amantes*, first by situating this book within her oeuvre as I read it and then by discussing the special problems posed in translating this work from French into English, moving whatever meaning it captures from the original into a framework that tends to impose a different set of discursive relations and a different construction of reality. In enunciative relations and referential operations, English calls for more precise and concrete determinations, for fuller, more cohesive delineations than does French.

Nicole Brossard has become well known as a lesbian feminist theorist and writer and as the leading figure among Quebec postmodernist writers. Her work blurs the boundaries between fiction and theory, subverting the fictions patriarchal discourse has spun about women's lives by working with the "re(her)alities" of women's lives that lie outside the codes of fiction. This exploration occurs principally in Brossard's "lesbian triptych," *L'Amèr* (*These Our Mothers*), *Le sens apparent* ("Surfaces of Meaning") and *Amantes (Lovhers)*. Together they demonstrate the many modes of experiencing and writing, the multiplicity Brossard sums up in the phrase, "The emotion of the thought/the thought of emotion." While *These Our Mothers* focuses on the thought of emotion, and *Le sens apparent* articulates the sensation of thought and emotion, *Lovhers* activates the emotion of thought.

"The Disintegrating Chapter," subtitle of *These Our Mothers*, points to the effect this feminist fiction has in dissolving the authority of the male tradition of the book. For it denounces the economics of proprietorship on which authorship is based, exposing the violence of both economic and literary codes of exchange which are based on the appropriation of matter. These are to be replaced by values of interdependence and multiplicity. Exploring the impact of the desiring female body on the body of language and on the text, Brossard sets up a "sapphic semantic chain" in which everything is turned upside down. Constituting a differential analysis of what it means to write as a woman from a position of deferred meaning outside the patriarchal symbolic order, wherein woman is represented (and disfigured) as Mother, Brossard's protagonist aims to enter the world of letters, to wrest control over her "cortex," her "body/text" and to escape from the contingency of matter imposed upon her through reproduction. She kills her womb, writes it, and is enfolded in the embrace of two identical yet different women, thus confounding the logical principle of identity.

This doubleness and paradox are compositional principles as well. Generic categories are blurred in the texts, which are exploratory, innovative, open. An emphasis on the activity of making sense results in production and process replacing reproduction and mimesis. Doubleness is created in grammar as well. Brossard's habit of ellipsis and parataxis creates multiple reference, while her neologisms and puns underline the multiplicity of meanings in each word, freeing them from clichés and customs. The community of multiple female bodies which decentres the concept of being is amplified in a multiplicity of female voices which disrupts the concept of the book. The loving allusions to women writers — Virginia Woolf, Colette — shared vocabulary and quotations, institute a feminist intertextuality, a matrilineal literary tradition.

The spiral is Brossard's figure for conveying the mobility and multiplicity, the indeterminacy, of the lesbian text. In its heart, where she writes, time opens onto Amazonian city time, island time and utopian time. Desire, memory and imagination are put into practice together, and they define the body on whose responsive vibrating surfaces (skin) the exploratory tongue makes sense. In lyrical descriptions of female desire, *Le sens apparent* develops feminist intertextuality in search of a locus for the lesbian text now that story-telling and representational detail have been excluded. Abandoning story or anecdote for "superimposition," Brossard makes her text overlap the story-telling of Adrienne and Gertrude and the short letters and random marks on paper written by Yolande. Adrienne and Gertrude, who have no patronyms, live in New York as well as in the fictional world of Yolande Villemaire whose work also explores the moving boundaries between fiction and reality, representation and sensation. But these word-beings may also have an extratextual life as Adrienne Rich and Gertrude Stein. This novel is thus located within the "spiral patterns in books written by women," adding another twist to these stories and establishing the basis for Brossard's depiction of writing as an act of loving and of the act of love as "the sense of touch which triggers desire: meditation."

Lovhers adds one more turn to this spiral, returning once again to New York. It is a study for the erotics of reading. To read this long poem alongside Adrienne Rich's New York suite, "Twenty-One Love Poems," situated in the same Amazonian city time, increases the connotative resonances. Paradoxically, the poetic sequence forms an ardent love letter to another woman. Their love-making in the Barbizon Hotel for Women is the central emotional core of the sequence. At the heart of the poem is an exploration of the erotics of reading which initiates the immemorial dialectics when memory, through quotations, teases out thought and launches the reader onto the associative drift which will effect the créative transformation into poem. As the epigraph announces, this is an example of "cerebral spinning." Shifting the emphasis from theory and the work on surfaces of the two earlier volumes, *Lovhers* concentrates on exploring various interconnecting modes of consciousness. In the fever of June, excitation is meditation on the communicative chain, the relation of sender, text, receiver, and on the desire which bonds them. Here Brossard writes of the way in which quotation and the fragment from a lover's text are the matrix for a new text. "The text of the project and the project of the text" are carried on in the "taste of words." This is a self-reflexive foregrounding of Brossard's own textual practice.

As the process of the project unfolds, it is caught up in a spiral of escalating desire and vertigo, moving variously through memory to explore the history of women's sensations during persecution in "My Memory of Love," succumbing to temptation, which is to pass through and to take on form. The sequence concludes with the visions of the imagination in the utopian time of "My Continent" where the categories of time and space are dissolved by the transforming word. Everything is confounded in a female continent inhabited by the loving and beloved voices of other lesbian writers.

To shift from interpretation to encoding, from reading to (re)writing, I shall begin with the history of this translation. Several sections of the sequence, including "The Temptation" and "My Continent," were translated for Brossard to read at "Writers in Dialogue" on May 1, 1981, in Toronto. On that occasion, Brossard was reading in counterpoint with Adrienne Rich. The poems were read aloud for an audience that knew little French and was not familiar with Brossard's work. In these circumstances, I opted to be a ventriloquist, to make the poems sound like Brossard's poems, and let the meaning take care of itself. To a certain degree, Brossard's text invites this type of transformation, since it is the associative drift of the sound of words that generates sequences.

10

Tone seeks out the word, sounds out the meaning. Traces of this initial translation are present in this version in such examples as "glaze and phrase" used to render "verre et du verbe" in "The Temptation" where a more literal rendering would be "glass and verb." Elsewhere, as in " July the Sea," I have let my ear determine my word choice, preferring in that poem the word "prolonging" over "extending" for the presence of the other word "longing" hidden within it.

What I am approaching here is the greatest difficulty facing the translator of Brossard's work, the great connotative wealth of each word on the page. The doubleness and multiplicity of meaning created through puns, ellipses and portmanteau words forces a new understanding of the limits of translatability. Given the requirement in English for more explicit and concrete determination than in French, and Brossard's practice of augmenting the indeterminacy of French referential operations, it is obvious that *Lovhers* is not *Amantes*. However, *Lovhers* effects its own work on language. While many of Brossard's puns such as the one on "délire," — both delirious associative drift and dé-lire, to unread or unfix reading — have been paraphrased and not translated, there are other plays on meaning that happen only in English, those relating to the word-cluster "sinks"-"ink" in "Igneous Woman," for example. With Brossard's neologisms which seek to disrupt our notions of gender in grammar, I have more often translated than paraphrased. Witness the assertion of the female presence in "amant*es*" as it has been transformed into "lov*h*ers." Granted there are fewer examples of this sort of grammatical play in *Lovhers* than in *These Our Mothers*. Another difference in the two books is the greater development of the lyric line in *Lovhers*. In this event, the necessity for greater concreteness imposed by English works accentuates the lyric flow. The paring down of language too, focuses attention on objects and on the female body, increasing the physicality of these erotic poems. Compare the juxtaposed "le café le midi la mer" in "July the Sea" to the more concrete "coffee noon sea." Brossard's focus on the desiring body thus emerges with greater clarity in English.

Enhanced too is her work on the material signifier, to foreground the physical reality of the activities of reading and writing — a

11

constant preoccupation in her work since the early seventies —
through typographical play on various typescripts and through the
focus on the white page which, along with interjected lines like
"turn the page," serve to draw the reader's attention to the fact
that she is reading only black marks on a white page and that the
meaning being produced is her own creation.

Reader, the pleasure of the text is now yours.

Barbara Godard

(4):
LOVHERS/WRITE

it celebrates cerebral spinning

Mary Daly

One of the festivals celebrated by the companion lovhers called a love festival may take many forms. Love festivals are generally a mutual celebration of two or more companion lovhers.

Monique Wittig
Sande Zeig

somewhere always a statement, skin concentrated
system inverted
attentive to the phases of love, this text
under the eye: June aroused by audacity
precise lips or this allurement of the clitoris
its unrecorded thought giving the body back intelligence
because each shiver aims at the emergence
June the fever the end of couples
their prolongation like the most unexpected of
silences: lesbian lovhers

the texture of identities

---

in reality, there is no fiction

"the rapture" said L. to grasp the sense
of a mental experience where fragments and delirium
from the explosion translate an experiment on riot
within the self as a theory of reality

rain prose simultaneously
a process which concentrates me through the lips
on your shoulder
urges the spasm
to become graphic: nothing tires our thighs
except a little gesture, a coincidence
that accompanies us for a long time the time
of a few decisive seconds:
moan so as to trace identity on the self
in the laboratory of emotions

I DON'T STOP READING/DELIRING
IN THIS JUNE OF LOVHERS

all my muscles this spiral
of your hands in the secret on my breasts

"Eye open to strange correspondences"
                    Michèle Causse

I DON'T STOP READING/DELIRING

according to the years of reality, imagine going from city to city to recite the smooth versions that slip into each body instigating the unfolding, the excitation: everywhere women kept watch in the only way plausible: beautiful and serious in their energy from spiral to spiral

— under the oranges of L.A. the frontier of fire between the ludicrous palm tree and the red flowers like aluminum foil. i am present at the accessible intersection of all the dangers which boost the current of compatible skins   excitation: what imperils reality, like an invitation to knowledge, integral presence

— near me, her fluid thought, ink,
her voice faintly seeking out words
a few feet away, our acts of
meditation face to face with writing
stretched out towards her with the same intensity
as my bending over her: breath

I DON'T STOP READING/DELIRING

"the splendour," said O.

"your strong tongue and slender fingers
reaching where I had been waiting years for you
in my rose-wet cave — whatever happens, this is."

Adrienne Rich

---

everywhere the project of cities and geographies to arouse our bodies to ever greater fluidity, endless flood into our mouths of savours makes this approach of delirium compatible with the mind and we imagine new customs with these same mouths that know how to make a speech, ours tasting of words tasting of kisses (i don't stop reading/deliring — excitation: what arouses the unrecorded in my skin)

"science" says Xa.
"lick to the heart of our vast plot"
                    Louky Bersianik

---

in the happy position of hands on hips a sexual tenderness runs throughout distances — fire is all we can see, the permanence of desire in our precision exercises because our searching lips captivate all our attention, called forth by the science of our music

June, the urgency of the fold: ramified couple holding in my hand a book by Djuna Barnes, I can't stop reading/deliring, i need all my tensions when confronting the drift because in all my muscles, a need for suppleness, that is when i make a spiral in front of you and when the strangest seduction takes form at the same time as the embrace.   tonight it seems night pushes us to behaviour which is sweetly desiring and our mouths are slowly extinguished, we can't be more attentive to their effects.

JUNE THE FEVER

i read the text of your project. i am writing you now from a sidewalk café on St. Denis where i have been sitting for an hour. it is a fine day and all about there is an air of reality. this café is called La Cour, it has a little yellow fence.

i don't know why, but rather than reading what you have written, i'd like to imagine it. i picture you obsessively in the midst of writing excessively as if nothing could stop you — so, you never worry about anything. when you quote, however, you must stop, it seems to me. for example, when you point out what Y observes: the relationship of thought to language is not a thing but a process, a continuous movement from thought to word and from word to thought, what happens in your eye?

i go at your project in pieces because literally it burns me. each fragment becomes my "integral" of you, the total work in the sense of an equivalence, of a shared reading facing the certainties i sometimes push away with tears, with forgetting or again with writing so as never to forget even if it is never entirely a question of memory: "a convenient fiction" to quote Murray whom you quote yourself.

reading the text of your project, i become aware of the extent to which our fictions intersect: looking in our respective circles for the statement of the theory and the theory of play which will put into motion the very emotion of motion.

the waitress just brought me another beer. of course, that doesn't interest you. however, in your text you write *and oriented toward action in everyday life*. i am obstinately looking for traces of everyday life in your work. nothing. everything is in the beyond. entirely real however in each of your gestures/totally abstract. sometimes i even pronounce "an abstraction" in your presence. you know however about my fever for everyday life and reality. my desire for words, my appetite for what allows me to imagine the real.

here i am trying to write by exploring all the mechanisms which serve to distract this i (permanent and unexplored) for you have clearly seen in your text of the project that nothing is written about identity without this motivation-mobile as is said about meaning on the look out or about meaning upended, turned back on itself. in reading you i am constantly seeking to displace myself in your words, to see them from all of their angles, to find areas of welcome there: *m'y lover, my love.*

if i am writing today it is so i can read you better provocatively so as to speak at last of the systems obsessing us: the brain produces its drugs which are our utopias.

three poets, three women who are poets have just sat down at the next table. i know them, we greet each other. *Picture theory*: these women and i are products of the same system. our albums of perception are full of complicity. we know the structure. but today, i stay alone at my table because i want to go on reading the text of your project.

i read your text and without second thought i note that you have written your name as a reference among others, with a publication date in parenthesis. i put the number (4) before inscribing *Lovhers* and i can only make headway by initials. just imagine a little what *fiction* might mean in these circumstances. an excess of realism compelled to be revealed only behind a screen of skin: mine. it's the tension demanded by any application of emotion. tension which gets a quality of attention. maybe there is a link with what you call the sources of ideological transformation.

my friends have left. there are some men, two i've spotted, who pass back and forth in front of the sidewalk café. they are crazy, i think. madness is on the loose here, scarcely noticed. i think they're all crazy. some are my age, others yours. their bodies are very *affected*. each madness has its own look, as if a crucial incident gives everyone's life, its *style*.

since 1972 you say, there has been a tendency to distinguish two types of content in long term memory: episodic and semantic. on that subject, i refer you back to *Prochain épisode* and *Trou de mémoire* by an author you probably don't know. they are books valuable for exploring what you call the "forms of consciousness".

i think all those books you surround yourself with excite you in a vital way. *me too*, mind you. as if each book produced emanations. we play then with the invisible.

seduced, carried away or touched to the quick. each time the strategy of the books must be unmasked and we leave foundering there in the course of the reading, our biological skins.

B.N. says in an interview (*exit*, winter 76-77): "certainly the volcano liberated Lowry, but something unusual happened, a simultaneous relationship between himself and his character, more than an identity, an exchange of personality... In fact, a passage from one to the other, from the writer into his writing until he actually confines himself, so that he is not liberated in the sense you say, but is put into his own inferno. There is an interview with Lowry where he is asked what he would like to write and he answers: Under, under, under the volcano."

that's the worst thing that could happen to me. it did happen to me. since then I haven't stopped reading/ deliring to climb back up to the surface, to find my surfaces again. which no doubt explains my obsession with surfaces of meaning.

i read the text of your project and i find it provocative. it takes spaces away from me. in what way is it important for you to understand the mechanisms of creativity? gap, uncertainty, excess, ellipsis. everything has to be transposed, doesn't it? especially don't confound the surfaces of meaning and the sense of this text. there is no confidence here though something is being confided to you. i said *text* but it may be a real letter. Y.V. says it plainly in the fire Episode of *La grande ourse*: "This text was written before it happened to me."

La Cour is full. a little girl is having fun picking up the plastic arrows they put in our glasses. i think she's very pretty. H. just came out of the Faubourg. in great shape.

when you quote Sullerot: ''Not just the dandies but also the 'lionesses'!'' what do you mean? has the thought of dying in venice crossed your mind? Your text of the project is full of this type of allusion: that excites me and you know it as on those evenings when you wait for my reaction and you are present, sober, at the metamorphosis. Sober and enraptured, already familiar with the place where you know how to put your hand so as to bring about the effect of reality: lovhers. while i am still trying to read/delirium.

i don't stop reading/deliring: ''After the first time 'i love you' doesn't mean anything'' — ''*Me too* is not a perfect answer, because what is perfect can only be formal, and form is missing here.''

you know if you want to get back to the feminine condition over which you pass so rapidly by the way, it increasingly takes the form of our liaison, that is to say the coherence there is between what you write and what i am writing.

you should say acknowledgement. W. and Z. whom you know, spent three years of their life recognizing the words one by one, not all of course, because some of them are unacceptable, unusable, at least in their present state.

i am telling you about my passion for reading you hidden behind these quotations. the facts are such that your

project of the text and the text of the project are com-
pleted in the taste of the words, in the taste of the kiss. i
know that you are real to me/therefore.

JULY THE SEA

*Since the day when the lesbian peo-
ples renounced the idea that it was
absolutely necessary to die, no one
has. The whole process of death has
ceased to be a custom.*

Monique Wittig
Sande Zeig

Emerging (Kay Gardner): noon *la mer*
METAPHOR'S splendour (4) from energy
rounded with desires/our progress
mouths: coffee noon sea
pretext origin of the kiss: taste
mobile in the full flood of memory _____ breath
and biographical shoulders emerging
like a process
the tides (at this level):
a reflex of rising tides

to find again every day life of lesbian
fictions of writing of obscurity and diurnal
the feel of tongues, the patience
of mouths devoting themselves to understanding
integral
body against thighs legato
only fever: the eye without its sighting

and thought takes shape
with suppleness in every sense
coincidence
concentrated in the island (4) loving women
picture theory/juillet la mer
voice the tongues' intention

from metaphor to rising tide
the versions
a form of perception my form
that founds the sounds
round us like letters
experimental
the tide amorous spiral
I run the risk of conquest
so as not to be non-sense

memory, some words are such
that an embrace conceives
their surfaces/allusions
because my obsession with reading
(with mouths) urges me
toward every discourse
round the generic sap
obsession tied to what questions
the abandon the conquest vulva wave
the tide of desire the keen defeat
of the writing fervent conquest: to read

july the sea is the provisional articulation
of pleasure which my sister brigand draws
our points of falling (emergency curves)
when <u>turning the page</u> means:
to follow
our reading binding our intentions like
a thought
issuing from this force *defeated*
inside our heads celebrating the reflex of vertigo
we can conceive anything

concrete within the fiction (wellspring
prolonging you)
from language and its folds
matter, all tides at the limit
in my temples are presented
skins of convocation in the prospect
of pacts _____ women reclining

feverish seaside coffee
scenario of what causes suffering
in the voices
how to describe this opera of the interior
passion like an overture
on the sea, a reflection
of the voice to arouse interest
illusion _____ lyre

last day on the island: amorous
rigour has assumed its sense and numbers
vigilant seductions assemble
for concentration (everything is so concrete,
orgasm like a process leading
to the integral: end of fragments
in the fertile progress of lovhers

IGNEOUS WOMAN, INTEGRAL WOMAN

autobiography or the appearance of facts
a few voices, i borrow from the dictionary
some mad laughter little by little, i'm dispersed
in the survived of things of the real
it's concentrated in the throb of life
in the integral skin of thought that
manifests

nothing sinks (however) night is passing
to dive head first into reality
such a compatible writing, its inks
i'm dispersed/multiple savour of lucidities

(bec.) the only reality
in body the (fiction) or this time
the mental space of the word women in ink
calls forth the unrecorded from myths and torment
turning point of the imaginary of forms of comfort

(i.e.) a spin in the bodies of docility
spiral lesbians by concentration (nape)

and if the biographies of fire
were advancing avalanche (like memory
unfolding its vertigoes)
identity upended in ecstasy

from the clamour of voices to anger
memory keeps watch in sounds
like an urging to spread out
over fogs this expression
of tear-filled eyes that have gone through
the arduous emotion of daily life
of complicity

i thought in profile and face to face
that nothing could put an end
to this skin of origin we know
splendidly in our territories
that this battle skin
knife undertow _____ eyes
that break up and bind turn amatory
phrases that address (letters)
women whose curves scintillate

this sleep (where everything began) of alerting
the woman who dreams in the abyss and the blank
sleep of deciphering (through which heat
passes) the skins of surface
in the folds and recesses and repetitions of patiences
each patience of our bodies is unprecedented
in its rhythm invents attraction
goes through our fists like a writing
an open signal

because the open veins of biographies
at top speed in our lives (because)
beside the suffering of foolish faults
of failure
rigour of the aside
all hunger like mad love
this probable imagination

(crisis) for me linked to words
(machine for divining symbols)
to the softness of lips, of eaux-de-vie
in the angle of neurological drifts

memory sketches from leaves and veins
with water all water
a monday morning of spiral in september
between the real and what flows from it
night is passing leading me
into the chemistry of the waters the women
pass through

because cities are circuses of dream
about which we think
since .... the obliqueness of fogs
in this expression we are speaking
integral, in the fog of avalanches
my woman, so that no cliché
separates us

MY MEMORY OF
(LOVE)

But remember. Make an effort to remember. Or, failing that, invent.

Monique Wittig

it begins (in) with the skin
if I want to stay in utopia
all love is working in me
and let's say amazes me
because the hypothesis *cyprine spring*
making i love you

(in the taxi leading to the Voyageur and to the Bread
and Puppet, let's concentrate on what could happen in
the present when our faculties succeed in producing cer-
tain embraces)
sunday afternoon

each time to remake the form of the womb
wind of velvet/the reply
the savour or again mental synthesis
time motivates words
I sometimes illustrate a few events

(among women, memory comes back like conscious-
ness//open me, tonight, it's all about our mouths and
our arms, and since it's all about us//open me)
saturday, *le silence magique*

to choose from memory what opens and is operative
unfurl *and the poem*
broaches biography, circles
(the fire) I am double to call up
a memory to satisfy
as harmony is written
as will itself is welcomed
water, Milan, your body: in the beginning

(the moon came up at the same time as a thousand
women got up, because the music)
friday, expressway

the beautiful muscular women in the grass
gratified and eager in pursuit have seen
their body hair glistening with a thousand arts
when memory came to them
from the surfaces, deep down, was born
the consciousness of space (with the women)

(i put on your perfume, in the circumstance i took ink
and silk road, for a few visions)
thursday, writing

attraction transforms experience and famous memory, remember *the th*imble (in your hand, around your finger or on the page) so each time into reality steals an image which meets your lips ready to speak. i want to tell you about the deliriums that ensue and the sobs and vertigo because then the body enters into tumult and paradox: if your memory fails

wednesday, madly in love

to torture one's style, to strain it into unnatural forms
to torture a text, to pervert it by transforming it, *to rack
one's brains*.

to torture: the memory of women is torrential when it's
a question of torture the ravage is great when torture is
thousands of years old and memory is short/*choppy like
a news item*/from alert from alarm sonorous sounding
device before being born sounded out
tuesday, anger

monday memory or again mental
synthesis, daily and absolute
through the window of the mirror, duration
(on this april monday i read all
day *reality begins with*
the intention of you
entirely
while i am working
on the window and on the mirror
the question of surfaces
of perspective

THE BARBIZON

writings make sense that begin with the declaration of love (*itself*) fixed in the heart of the century and of subterranean proliferating and vociferating mythologies of voices caught in the cliché, cities, (*in play*)

The Barbizon Hotel for Women

an intuition of reciprocal knowledge
women with curves of fire and eiderdown
fresh-skinned — essential surface
you float within my page she said
and the four dimensional woman is inscribed
in the space between the moon and (fire belt)
of the discovery and combats that the echo
you persevere, fervour flaming

mouth diffuse, nocturnal and intimate
round with intervals
to pass through the gardens of the real
anticipated paintings of the attentive body
all the regions of the brain
time is measured here in waters
into vessels, in harmony
the precision of graffiti in our eyes
fugitives (here) the writings
in THE BARBIZON HOTEL FOR WOMEN
nascent figures within the wheel
cyclical tenderness converging

space (mâ)
among all ages, versatile
wrinkles of the unexpected woman
when midnight and the elevator
in us rises the fluidity
our feet placed on the worn out carpets
here the girls of the Barbizon
in the narrow beds of America
have invented with their lips
a vital form of power
to stretch out side by side
without parallel and: fusion

but the napes of our necks attentive when
on Lexington Avenue steps
move close to us again
because *the scene* is memory
and the memory within our pages
explodes
like a perfect technique
around this eccentric passion
we imagine in the beautiful grey
chignons of the women of the Barbizon

so transform me, she said
into a watercolour in the bed
like a recent orbit
the curtains, the emotion
tonight we are going to the *Sahara*

we are walking into the abstract (neons)
tonight — overexposed — unfettered expression
nocturnal women
my reflex and the circumstances
which my mouth walks like words
i expose myself: a useful precaution
sur terre: down town
amazons have studios for correspondence

and here again i find *an author too abstract*
supplicating in space
body itself intensity
and the rain suddenly
abundant
to reunite intuitions of matter

the embraces _____ the extent of thought
in the grass i'll be quick to take
the silk road
with a tongue that has visions
it is essential to hold back: presence/
on the verge of

space (mâ) memory round with vowels
with ultimate certainty without respite

The Temptation

i succumbed to all the visions
seduced, surface, series and serious
in all mobility and landscapes
concentrated on each episode
territory and cheek. masked/unmasked:
hors l'espace or full of intonations
in the climate delirious around
all the figures, aerial
in the use of glaze and phrase

i succumbed to the fury, the cities
and the etchings/come/the
conversation in snatches, in the open
the entire palm imprint of slowness
and reality transforms its lynx
eyes of identity which motivate
all the resources the tongue braids
existence by dint of constant courses
and breath within the limits of the possible
of the tolerable blindly: feeling

i succumbed to the clear vision
of vegetation and events
of early morning, in the privileges of light
because the authentic body spine of fire
has shown its tongue as it
was then tangible and tango
very vivid for the eyes/of the inside

i succumbed to the temptation as
one enters the round of gestures
ensuring survival, conquest
smile and fusion of fictions
the night come when the bangs
our foreheads remember the most delightful
delinquencies, the hand is moved a bit
so that before our eyes opens up
the agile memory of utopian girls
moving in italics
or in a fresco towards all the issues

i succumbed to the impression and instantaneous
both of us ----- life mobilizes itself
with the fine ardour of women showing forth
their vertigo and those two
dazzled *sur terre* turning seized suddenly
in the most ritual amorous slownes s ex---
temptation with all gravity
of ecstasy, these two were so
enraptured celebrating the daily
emergence of temptation

i succumbed to the echo, the rebound
to the repetition. *in the beginning
of the vertebrae* was the duration
an essential rejoinder at every instant
in the joy I have in you, lived
duration of signs, stricken
with collusion and the waters
of reading and delirium
the agility of thighs each time
surprises me in space because they are
this opening originated at all
times in all vegetation
the vitality of cycles: our images

i succumbed attentively to the very
point of knowing that for each
temptation a meaning must be preserved: *recollected*
and *resumed* ----------- to open onto mental
space, with words of lightning, sequence
of unreason, episode of recommencements
and of breasts unrecorded web: the mouths
science of the real, skin/itinerary
going away to slip gently
into the continent of women

i succumbed: that's what drags me
into the real and vertigo at the same time
into the surrounding grasses (they touch
our most sensitive tissues)
------ eclipses ------
temptation beyond words
to devise an architecture
when everything veers towards fever so
even a clever description:
moving me towards the other woman
unanimous
other than *naturally*

i succumbed even unto the certainty
which designates the initial legend
the one that excavates the passed'n time
and prompts the question
of distance *(itself)* in the fire of
fictions/to succumb becomes thus to pass through
take shape and choose oneself
a consent affecting the woman in love

The Vision

any vision is essentially mathematical from imaginary
space. it carries within itself the evidence, the vital
form that grows from the ardour to which we succumb
through passion. through necessity or through excess

vertigo 1

she says that from the top of the buildings the city can
scarcely be seen on some days and that is when she can
feel certain sensations which refresh her and give her: a
special relish for civilization. she repeats all around her
that cities are avalanches which sweep down on us emit-
ting sounds inaudible to all except women. she is con-
stantly experiencing the city in everything ludicrous the
city throws at women caught without shopping bags.
she takes her inspiration from the tang of the sea each
time the city begins to revolve under its long buildings as
if the city were calling as it dived the wrong way round,
without the real form of what nourished it appearing.
she often stretches out her arms to touch the *guard*/
rails though she knows they are always there she grap-
ples then with the question of vertigo

2

about vertigo and its form, what relates to the confines
of conflicts, but about vertigo or about surfaces: caught
in a whirlwind, believing that everything is turning
around her without understanding why she isn't turn-
ing. presumes then that the universe is cycle and rota-
tion. but contrary to her expectations, the world files
off/before her in a completely straight line according to
the law of patriarchal heritage. in motion, and perceives
that nothing around her is turning: caught then in
inconceivable vertigo

3

in the space full of reflections: unprecedented vertigo.
dizzy/tempted/and/enraptured. all her senses are work-
ing for her to give her pleasure and to make her think up
a version of existence which takes a displacement of the
horizon for granted. it is only since she has become vigi-
lant that she can see for herself that *conventional ver-
tigo* has given way to dazzling

4

complete, or again the palm
very evidently the trace of events
burns straight into (complete) integrity
which the arms supply around
this smile
and mobile, how do you say
modern, each time
i assume the entire fiction
taking place there, and substitution

spiral 1

in her hand she holds a post card on which the moon can
be seen faintly, mountainous shapes and in the centre, a
spiral that is neither galaxy, nor nautilus, nor an optical
illusion. right in the heart of Manhattan, as though
fixed by certainty or by a vision. all around her, women
are turning pages, reading, buying books — Je veux
acheter un livre — she thinks there is no such thing as
chance but rather collusion in the exploration of forms
and that this one aims to tell the *essenshe'll* about the
spatial era of women

2

spatial, initial, irrigate the inside of the tissues, the skin
rises up, i am seeking completion _____
to continue in acts of drifting and of the visible, the ten-
sions present in certain inscriptions when emotion anti-
cipates in such a way that roots are tangled, stubborn-
ness from the allure of conquest, the setting to work of
ultimate possibles

3

it's in space: figure and i add landscape/everything is inverted/i give myself up to the recommencement of the act face to face with language as in the beginning of the inversion of identities. to concentrate myself upon the essential agitation or myself dispersed like multiple connections touching my whole surface, the limits. to persist so memory, after that

4

add also the experience inflicted on women's bodies urges toward reality _____ this prolonged silence but obvious trace of the spiral in position, contemporary and radical. something is brooding somewhere in this century: about thought or about the absurdity of the species. *(what) species of woman* is coming showing the tip of a breast as though to signal the beginning of a cycle. if nobody moves in this instant everything can vertigo to become virtual

sleep 1

that's when we find the two women again in the narrow bed of the BARBIZON HOTEL FOR WOMEN reclining totally exhausted, they investigate sleep like a space where the inner rhythm releases processes of initiation to lightning, to ellipsis, *to gender*. night, the city, drowsy in the unthought of the *poem*, in the proximity of enigmas to reunite the signs so ------- that are used to maintain life, to move away from it. doubled by the startled bodies, agreeing to the awakening

2

cannot imagine the experience of sleep otherwise than through what acquiesces in me of a reflexion, then the enthusiasm, music that knots the space of the window between my eyebrows and your soft skin settling into me like wisdom. sleep must be pushed to the limit

3

the arrow of water in the soul, in our night visions there
is *this excess* which encourages discernment. by the
voice of a thousand spectacles in us, we swallow the
reality that substitutes itself for the imaginary. thus
sleep as a meditation. you give me intense reality or ob-
scure integrity to come from the remotest regions: to
take its place

4

so sensitive when the skin lends itself and when we
are gifted for certain sparse words in bed that mouths
give up at dayfall ------- successively it is crossed by a
dream, entwined women, in the least detail branches out
and compromises itself ---- some appeasement, the echo
deferred, dispersal, the night declines its relays. to
explore: the ultimate intimate elsewhere

excess 1

she is drunk (dead), in a final leap (19th century with
absinth) and with scotch/Sahara/agile (because
women's voices are the surroundings) she sometimes
thinks between two spirals that excess is her double and
her strength. all opportunities are real in the face of
intensity: even more so in the face of intelligence. to
understand the intent that loosens the vocal cords of
childhood in the feminine. she crosses Lexington, know-
ing the limits; that is when she exhausts reflexion, fun-
damentally very double: with

2

the head turns, let us hug the details of our science,
bound women (the ultimate intimate elsewhere) per-
ceiving that from the private all excess/sinks/ because
THE (male) politics of the gaze of sexual bliss is also the
silence of bodies elongated by hunger, fire, dogs, the
bite of densities of torture and the head turns from all
the excesses which the members of the dismembered
body add to the unambiguous silence of the sexual bliss
we know: women converging

3

audacity: to move out of the body going from the intimate to the political, keeping its vital flow and its topography without making excess that ex arm drama burning reality with its white acid. the exercise of excess in the feminine of lips and fists participates in this cerebral accompaniment which the skin of emotion engenders in the most plausible spatial equation

4

hope to say I desire: but never get beyond the political (because of the curves). i insist on making visible the agitation which is outlined there. my excesses: the intention of all the sources of excess like access to the source. with regard to us, a memory/real duration because history has its reasons and the skin paradise stays tenacious and becomes wet

MY CONTINENT

MY *continent* she now has
all my saliva, since, at your place, i've
forgotten the text i wanted before your
reading eyes which have watched centuries
of hallucinations, of skin, pass, the noise/
detonation. (mâ)* it's a space/an hypothesis

* mâ — japanese term for space
  ma — possessive pronoun, feminine gender in French

my continent woman of all the spaces
cortex and flood: a sense of gravity
bringing me into the world
my different matter into existence which
fills and drains this *singular* tension
like the ultimate vitality and
wisdom where intelligence and breasts, thighs
one after the other sleeping and agitation
breasts get the better of breath
we find there/writing

my continent of spaces of reason and
(of love) like a history of space
where we can speak concretely
about allegiance and caresses in silence
a form of reverberation/i cut across
cities without simulating *nature* because
i'm so civilized before the sea
at flood tide, persistent/i read
"The whole sea goes toward the city"
and also in your language
"Non smettete di delirare, questo è il
momento de l'utopia"

my continent multiplied by those who have signed:
Djuna Barnes, Jane Bowles, Gertrude Stein, Natalie
Barney, Michèle Causse, Marie-Claire Blais, Jovette
Marchessault, Adrienne Rich, Mary Daly, Colette and
Virginia, the other drowned ones, Cristina Perri Rossi,
Louky Bersianik, Pol Pelletier, Maryvonne so attentive,
Monique Wittig, Sande Zeig, Anna d'Argentine, Kate
Millett, Jeanne d'Arc Jutras, Marie Lafleur, Jane Rule,
Renée Vivien, Romaine Brooks
to write: the real/the skin clairvoyant
pupil essential in the unfolding
of my consciousness and expression: my double
a singular mobility and the continent
indeed a joy

my continent, i mean to talk about the radical
effect of light in broad daylight
today, i've held you close,
loved by every civilization, every
texture, every geometry and ember,
delirious, as it is written: and
my body is enraptured

By the Same Author

POETRY

«Aube à la saison» in *Trois* (1965).
Mordre en sa chair (1966).
L'écho bouge beau (1968).
Suite logique (1970).
Le Centre blanc (1970).
Mécanique jongleuse (1973).
Mécanique jongleuse suivi de *Masculin gramaticale* (1974).
La Partie pour le tout (1975)
Le Centre blanc (Collection Rétrospective, 1978).
D'Arcs de cycle la dérive (1979).
Amantes (1980).
Double Impression (Collection Rétrospective, 1984).
L'Aviva (1985).
Domaine d'écriture (1985).
Dont j'oublie le titre (1986).

PROSE

Un livre (1970, 1980).
Sold/out (étreinte/illustration) (1973, 1980).
French kiss (étreinte/exploration) (1974, 1980).
L'Amèr ou Le Chapitre effrité (1977).
Le Sens apparent (1980).
Picture theory (1982).
Journal intime (1984).
La lettre aérienne (1985).

THEATRE

«L'écrivain» in *La nef des sorcières* (1976).

Printed in Canada